LEADER'S GUIDE

Yes, No, Maybe So

Dealing with Doubt

Jeff Munroe

CRC Publications
Grand Rapids, Michigan

ACKNOWLEDGMENTS

CRC Publications is grateful to Jeff Munroe for writing this course. A pastor in the Reformed Church in America, Munroe is associate regional director for Young Life in the Great Lakes region.

The Scripture quotations in this publication are from the HOLY BIBLE, NEW INTERNATIONAL VERSION, © 1973, 1978, 1984, International Bible Society. Used by permission of Zondervan Bible Publishers.

Yes, No, Maybe So
Dealing with Doubt

LifeWise
© 1996 CRC Publications
2850 Kalamazoo Ave. SE
Grand Rapids, MI 49560

All rights reserved.
Printed in the United States of America on recycled paper. ✪

ISBN 1-56212-163-4

10 9 8 7 6 5 4 3 2 1

Contents

Introduction 5
Meeting 1   Is Doubt Our Enemy? 9
Meeting 2   What Is Faith, Anyway? 15
Meeting 3   Looking for Answers? 21
Meeting 4   What's Our Focus? 27
            Leader Evaluation Form 33

Introduction

LIFEWISE

Life for today's young people is increasingly complex and confusing. Through this series, we want to help high school youth find a basic frame of reference for living in this sometimes difficult world. By inviting teens to openly and actively express their faith, both in word and in deed, we can help them become a positive force for change in their complex world of work, school, and society.

Our goals for this series are as follows:

- to promote a healthy discussion of life issues
- to develop a biblical and Reformed perspective on life issues
- to make choices that are rooted in God's Word
- to grow in our personal commitment to live as God's people in a secular culture

Yes, No, Maybe So is part of the LifeWise series for high school youth. Each course in the series offers four sessions dedicated to issues that are important to young people. The courses include a complete leader's guide with step-by-step instructions for leading group meetings and a book of perforated handouts.

These courses are intended to create a forum for discussion of important issues. You, as group leader, will be facilitating that discussion as together your group addresses different problems. You will encourage group members to think critically about where they stand personally in relation to these issues and about how their Christian life affects the way they act and live on a day-to-day basis.

GOALS AND CONTENT

The goals of *Yes, No, Maybe So: Dealing with Doubt* are as follows:

- to realize that doubt is an inevitable (and even integral) part of faith
- to evaluate the role of faith in our lives
- to begin to address our own questions and doubts
- to build up our faith by keeping Jesus at its center

The four meetings of this course deal with the following themes:

- Meeting 1 introduces the idea of doubt as a normal human experience that doesn't have to produce guilt or cause us to lose our faith. We look at some of the reasons why John the Baptist doubted, even though he knew Jesus personally. And we list some of the questions we would like to ask Jesus if we could.

- Meeting 2 helps us look at the meaning and place of faith in our lives. We look at a contemporary version of Jesus' encounter with a rich young man. We talk about some of the stumbling blocks that can get in the way of our faith.

- Meeting 3 offers an opportunity to list some of our own questions and to begin to address them honestly and rationally. We'll look at Doubting Thomas and realize that God wants us to search for answers to our questions and that answers are available. At the same time we must trust his handling of issues that are beyond our understanding.

- Meeting 4 reminds us that living with our doubts is possible if we keep our eyes on Jesus and make him the center of our faith. From the story of Peter walking on water toward Jesus, we'll draw conclusions about our own faith. And we'll identify specific ways to help ourselves focus on Jesus.

MATERIALS

To lead the course you'll need this leader's guide and a book of handouts for yourself and one for each group member. The leader's guide and handouts are explained in more detail below.

You'll also need Bibles, paper and pencils or pens, markers, and a pad of newsprint or other large sheets of paper. Check the *Materials* list of each meeting for any other items needed to lead the session.

AUDIENCE AND GENERAL APPROACH

This course is designed for four discussion-based meetings and is intended for use by high school youth. It can be used in church school, youth group, or retreat settings.

Ideally you should have a full hour for each of the four meetings. You'll find there are plenty of activities to fill sixty minutes or more. Should you have less time, you'll need to trim or even omit some suggested steps. But be sure not to settle for less than forty-five minutes per meeting.

This course uses many small group activities. They're lively and fun, and they help participants learn from each other. They are designed to encourage participants to delve into each issue, to think deeply about how each issue affects their lives, and to discuss each issue from a Christian perspective.

LEADER'S ROLE

As leader, your main tasks are the following:

- to get to know each group member
- to keep the various activities moving and on track
- to facilitate discussion and interaction
- to model what it means to be open to God's Word and Spirit

Try to cultivate an atmosphere of openness that allows each person to feel free and secure. Think of yourself as a colearner with the group, a fellow traveler on a journey of faith.

To prepare for each meeting, carefully read through the leader's guide material. This material is explained for you below.

USING THE LEADER'S GUIDE

This leader's guide will help you prepare for and lead the meetings. It will tell you when and how to use the handouts that accompany this course.

Scripture
Here you'll find the Scripture passages used during the meeting.

Today's Theme
This brief introductory section is intended to start you thinking about the day's theme and what the issue at hand means for your group.

Goals of the Meeting
Each meeting plan provides a set of goals that you can refer to throughout your meeting time to keep your discussion on track. These goals should constitute a guideline for your meeting, not a strict rule. We encourage you to add goals as needed to fit the needs and interests of the teens in your group.

Materials
This section lists all the materials you'll need for the meeting, including any materials you'll need for warm-up group activities.

Theme Thoughts
This section is designed to give you, as leader, a deeper biblical/theological perspective on the issue you're addressing in the meeting. Please resist any impulse to lecture to the group on this section's contents. It's just for you.

Meeting Plan (Steps)
Different every meeting, these steps are designed to give you interesting and "active" methods for reaching the goals of the meeting. Some of these steps use the handouts, others do not.

Options
These optional activities are intended to increase your flexibility in leading your group and to stimulate your creativity. Substitute these steps for others in the meeting plan when and if you feel that the option would be more meaningful or appealing to your group members.

Handouts
You should order a book of perforated handouts for each group member and for yourself. Prior to each meeting time, tear the necessary handouts from each book and have them ready to distribute at the appropriate time.

The handouts are used during the meetings for a variety of activities. They contain prompts for biblical study, group activities, surveys, and other material. Handouts are numbered sequentially throughout the course.

ADDITIONAL SUGGESTIONS FOR LEADERS

Be personal!
First, be personal in the sense of being yourself. Don't try to be something you normally aren't. Most teens can immediately see through an adult who is trying to be "cool" just to impress them. Be yourself, and act your age.

Second, be personal in the sense that you respect each young person for who he or she is, for the strength of his or her character, and for the ability to reason and apply what he or she is learning through these meetings.

Third, be personal in the way you see yourself: as a leader but also as a colearner with the group. Let them know you don't have all the answers, that you are on a faith journey *with* them.

Don't be afraid to say "I don't know" or "I'm not sure" or "Help me think that through, will you?" Applying our Christian principles to issues can be difficult and perplexing—for adults as well as for young people.

Be a good listener
Resist the temptation to do all of the talking yourself (otherwise known as lecturing). Learn to be a good listener, even if it means patiently enduring times of silence. Give group members time to think and to respond. Show by your comments and your body language that you appreciate their contributions (even if you don't agree with everything they say).

When you do ask questions, remember to keep a good balance of questions of *fact*, questions of *opinion* or interpretation, and questions of *foundations*. The last category of questions asks people to explain the basis on which they have made their judgments. An important part of your task is to help your group recognize the value of basing their judgments on Scripture and on the teachings of the church.

Look for and take advantage of opportunities for your group members to take responsibility for the meeting's activities. In doing so you'll provide them with a sense of ownership for the group discussion and activities.

Be creative
Use this material to guide—not dictate—your discussion. Adapting the discussion topics and activities to better suit your situation should be your goal as a group leader. We offer several alternative steps at the end of each meeting plan to allow you more flexibility and choice in leading your meetings.

You may find that each meeting has more material in it than you can cover in the time you have available. Feel free to pick and choose between the steps, the options at the end of the meeting plan, and your own ideas. Make it *your* meeting, tailored to the needs and interests of *your* group.

Have fun!
Learning is meant to be enjoyable. God calls us to enjoy him and to celebrate his goodness. Reflect that celebration in your setting. If you are confined to a room at church, avoid placing the chairs in an arrangement that looks and feels like school. Use the games and other exercises not only to learn together but also to laugh together.

EVALUATION FORMS

At the end of this guide is a leader's evaluation form for you to complete. An evaluation form for group members is included in the handouts for this course. You can help us improve this series by completing these forms.

Please send completed evaluation forms to

LifeWise
CRC Publications
2850 Kalamazoo Ave. SE
Grand Rapids, Michigan 49560

MEETING 1
Is Doubt Our Enemy?

SCRIPTURE

Luke 3:1-22; 7:18-23

TODAY'S THEME

Where does doubt fit into the life of faith? Is doubt the opposite of faith, or is it an inevitable (and even integral) part of having faith?

As their cognitive abilities develop, young people are increasingly able both to imagine God and to question God. A young person may have an idea or a thought about God, and then believe he or she is the first ever to think such a thing. At times, this can produce guilt ("I shouldn't think this about God"), or it can cause young people to question and even abandon their faith ("I can't believe in a loving God who lets innocent people suffer").

This meeting introduces the concept of doubt as a normal human experience that doesn't have to produce guilt or cause us to lose our faith. Try to create an open environment in which kids are free to ask their questions and express their doubts. In our consumer-oriented culture, we need a measure of skepticism and doubt to survive. While doubt is not necessarily an asset in the life of a believer, its presence does suggest an active mind and faith. Some saints have progressed to a level where they have such a real awareness of the presence of God that doubt plays very little part in their faith. But a young person who "has no doubts" may not have a genuine faith either.

GOALS OF THE MEETING

- to understand that God created us with the ability to doubt, and that doubt is necessary to live successfully in our culture
- to describe how and why John the Baptist doubted, even though he knew Jesus personally
- to list questions we would ask Jesus if we could

MATERIALS

1. Bibles
2. Handouts 1-3, pens or pencils
3. A tabloid newspaper (the more bizarre the better)
4. One popular magazine for every two group members

THEME THOUGHTS

Film producers speak of "suspending disbelief," in other words, forgetting what one knows to be true. Good films are very effective at causing people to suspend their disbelief. Over the past few years, audiences have temporarily believed that the actor Tom Hanks was a lawyer with AIDS, a slow-but-wise Southerner, and a heroic Apollo astronaut. Even though we *know* the person we're watching is really Tom Hanks, we get so caught up in the movie that we stop thinking of him as Tom Hanks.

Although we rightly think of the ability to have faith as something God has given us, it is possible we were created more inclined to disbelief than belief. That's why filmmakers and other creative people work so hard at suspending our disbelief. If we were to watch the movie *Apollo 13* and think, "Tom Hanks sure does look goofy in that spacesuit," the film would have been a flop. Instead it was a hit, because when we watched it, we saw the character Jim Lovell, not the actor Tom Hanks.

It is easy to believe in things we can see and touch. We believe in chairs, for example, and throw our bodies onto them with abandon. We can see that a chair looks as if it will support us, and we have had a lifetime of successful experiences with chairs. So when we want to sit, and a chair is handy, we plop down without a second thought.

It gets harder with unseen things. How do we know that the things we can't see, like love or hope or God, are real? As someone once said, "If love is real, send me a box of it." Part of being human is wondering about unseen things. Sometimes people speak of "feeling God's presence," but often many of us don't feel anything. And when we do feel something, we wonder if it's really God or just an overactive imagination.

During this meeting, you and your group will consider John the Baptist's experience with doubt. John's mission in life was to prepare the way for the Messiah. When Jesus came forward, John pointed him out and had the incredible experience of baptizing the Son of God. Standing in the Jordan River, John saw the Spirit of God descend on Jesus in the shape of a dove. Then he actually heard the voice of God say, "This is my Son, whom I love; with him I am well pleased" (Matt. 3:17).

Even after all these experiences, Luke reports that John wondered if Jesus really was the Messiah (Luke 7:18 ff.). Because John had been arrested and was sitting in prison, he had plenty of time to reflect on all the events he had witnessed. Periodically, he would also receive updates on what Jesus was doing. Knowing that he would probably soon be executed, John wondered if he had gotten it right when he called Jesus the Messiah. He wanted to die with the certainty that he had not made a mistake on the mission he'd been sent to fulfill. Why, John wondered, didn't Jesus do the things the Messiah was supposed to do?

John had the opportunity to have his questions taken directly to Jesus and answered immediately. Wouldn't it be wonderful to be able to do that?

MEETING PLAN

1 TABLOID MANIA
5 minutes

Pick up an outlandish supermarket tabloid newspaper—the kind with headlines about space aliens with seven heads and Elvis working at Burger King. Have a few laughs showing the kids the headlines and the pictures. Ask if the group thinks anyone believes what is written in these kind of tabloids. Why do people read them?

2 WHAT DO YOU BELIEVE?
10-15 minutes

This exercise is similar to the previous one, but in a somewhat more subtle dimension. Divide the group into pairs, and give each pair a popular magazine (such as *People, Time, Maclean's,* or *Sports Illustrated*). Ask each pair to look through their magazine and find one advertisement that makes claims they doubt are really true.

You may want to show a sample ad that makes claims you don't believe. Point out how the whole ad—including pictures, colors, words—creates the message that "using this product will make your life better." For example, using one kind of toothpaste will make you irresistible to the opposite sex; wearing a certain brand of athletic shoe will enhance your game; a luxury sedan will give you prestige.

Also ask the pairs to choose an ad that they like and believe. Give them five minutes to go through their magazine, and then ask them to report what they've found.

Discuss the difference between the believable and unbelievable in advertising, using questions like these:

- Are we more inclined to believe or disbelieve the claims of advertisers? (Having been raised in this culture, we approach advertising with a high degree of sophistication. Although we enjoy the more creative ads and are occasionally moved by various ads, the older we get, it seems, the more skeptical we are of advertising claims.)
- What are some other statements you've heard recently that you doubted or wondered about? (If group members need help, suggest such areas as promises made by politicians, predictions about the future, statements made by a radio or TV talk show host, information about history presented by a film or video, threats by a person in authority, and so on.)
- Do you agree or disagree that doubt is necessary for survival in today's society? (Talk about how naive, overly-trusting individuals can easily become victims of rip-off schemes, fraud, and phonies of every imaginable kind. Not that we should doubt everyone and everything—that's cynicism. But in a deceitful world we do need to ask, and ask repeatedly, "Is this true? Can he or she be trusted?")

3 JOHN, THE WILD AND WOOLLY

20 minutes

Distribute Handout 1 ("John, the Wild and Woolly") to each group member. Read the introductory paragraphs to the group:

Of all the characters in the Bible, John the Baptist may be the most colorful. He lived in the desert, wore a camel-hair shirt (talk about itchy!), and ate locusts (better known as caterpillars) and wild honey. Not only would it take a whole lot of honey to make a locust taste good, but chances are John didn't bother getting the bees out of the way when he dipped into the honey.

People were drawn to John in large numbers. Some probably came out of curiosity, but others were attracted by what he had to say. He was flat-out committed to telling the truth, and he let the high and mighty have it with both barrels.

We'll look at two momentous events in John's career: first, when Jesus comes to John and asks to be baptized; second, when John is in jail and wonders if Jesus really is the Messiah.

Have the kids take turns reading the story of Jesus' baptism (Luke 3:1-22). Then discuss questions 1-2. Guidelines follow:

1. Put yourself in John's position when he baptized Jesus. How would you feel if Jesus came to you asking to be baptized? Why?

Listen to the various suggestions. Imagine how we'd feel if, say, a world leader showed up at our house for supper, seeking our blessing on his work. Like John, we'd probably feel happy and proud, but also unworthy, humble, nervous. Contribute your own feelings to the discussion.

You may want to ask someone to read Matthew's account of Jesus' baptism (Matt. 3:13-15). This passage clearly shows John's reluctance to baptize Jesus, one who was infinitely greater than John.

2. What kind of Messiah does John expect Jesus to be?

In verses 16 and 17 we see that John expects Jesus to be a fiery, powerful leader who would use his winnowing fork to "gather the wheat into his barn, but . . . burn up the chaff with unquenchable fire." Ask someone what they think this picture means. John saw Jesus as a farmer sifting wheat (those who repented) from chaff (those who did not repent). He expected the Messiah to be a man of action who would bring swift judgment to the unrepentant while providing safety and security for his followers.

Have group members read Luke 7:18-23. Continue discussing the questions.

3. **Imagine John sitting alone in prison. What do you think is going through his mind? What do the two disciples tell him?**

What would be more likely to make you reflect on your life than being in prison, knowing you will probably be executed? Perhaps John wonders if all his efforts to prepare the way for the Messiah were successful. Perhaps he's thinking about what Jesus was doing, wondering when and how he would bring the judgment that John spent so much time warning people about. No doubt John is eager for news from the outside world.

Then two of John's disciples come and tell him about all the wonderful things Jesus is doing (have your group look back at the first part of Luke 7 to find out what these things were).

4. **What question does John want his disciples to ask Jesus? Why would he want them to ask such a question?**

John wants the disciples to ask Jesus, "Are you the one who was to come, or should we expect someone else?" In other words, Are you really who you say you are? Are you the promised Messiah?

At first, John's question seems strange. Hasn't the experience of baptizing Jesus provided John with enough evidence to answer that question? Has John lost faith in Jesus? Or has he never had faith in Jesus? Has he run out of patience, waiting for Jesus to assert himself as Messiah?

Most likely, John's question arises because he is puzzled by what Jesus is doing. Instead of bringing judgment to the world, Jesus is busy doing works of mercy.

5. **Jesus gives John a strange answer. What six things does Jesus say characterize his ministry?**

Jesus asks John's disciples to report what they have seen and heard: the blind receive sight, the lame walk, those who have leprosy are cured, the deaf hear, the dead are raised, and the good news is preached to the poor. These deeds of love and mercy are a definite contrast to John's expectations of the Messiah bringing judgment to the people.

6. **To better understand Jesus' answer, look up Isaiah 29:18-19; 35:5-6; and 61:1, passages that John knew very well. What might John have thought, hearing this answer from Jesus?**

The Old Testament parallels show that Jesus' healing miracles and preaching to the poor have messianic significance. Jesus did not fit the popular Jewish notion of the Messiah as a powerful, liberating conqueror who would lead a revolt. According to Jesus, the Messiah's work would be accomplished through deeds of mercy, not through a political overthrow.

Jesus' answer does two things for John—it instructs him in the true nature of the Messiah, and it relieves John's doubt.

7. **In what ways are we like John? Different from John? What can we learn from John's experience?**

Even those who were physically close to Jesus had questions and moments of doubt. Sometimes we think, "It would be so easy to believe in Jesus if we had seen him do his miracles." But here is John, who saw the heavens open and heard God's own voice, experiencing doubt.

John wasn't sure about Jesus because Jesus wasn't acting the way he thought the Messiah would act. How often do we question God when events don't happen the way we think they should? Our preconceptions, prejudices, and expectations often cause us to question or doubt. Instead of giving up our pet ideas, we stubbornly cling to them.

Jesus doesn't overwhelm John's disciples. He answers their question gently and indirectly by describing what he has done. Rather than forcing us to believe, he lets us draw our conclusions about who he is.

4 YOUR QUESTIONS
10 minutes

As the discussion winds down, distribute Handout 2 ("Your Questions"). Ask each person to imagine that he or she has the opportunity John the Baptist had to ask Jesus anything. What would they ask? Give group members several quiet minutes to reflect and write. Be sure to complete the exercise yourself. Then call the group together.

Ask for volunteers to share their questions with the group. You may want to start by sharing one or two of your own responses.

Some questions may be funny or outlandish, but others may be poignant. Try to convey an open attitude that allows all questions—including those that express doubt—to be freely expressed and discussed. You may want to write the questions on a sheet of newsprint for reference throughout the course.

If there's time, talk about one or two of the questions today (you'll have another opportunity to discuss them at length in meeting 3). Let the group sense that you regard their questions as very important. In any discussion, avoid the temptation to offer quick answers. Let the kids talk about the questions from their perspective.

These questions can help you as a leader by giving you a better sense of where your group members are on their spiritual journeys. Perhaps you can use the questions to shape the direction of future topics of study for your group. Or you could offer to talk to anyone who wishes to discuss his or her own spiritual journey with you.

5 CLOSING
5-10 minutes

Close by reading the following quote from Frederick Buechner (Handout 2):

Whether your faith is that there is a God or that there is not a God, if you don't have any doubts, you are either kidding yourself or asleep. Doubts are the ants in the pants of faith. They keep it awake and moving.

Ask group members what they think Buechner means by "Doubts are the ants in the pants of faith."

Comment that God wants us to express our feelings—even when they include doubts—to him in prayer, as David does in Psalm 77. Distribute Bibles, divide into two groups, and read the first nine verses responsively.

Invite everyone to spend a couple of minutes in silent prayer expressing his or her feelings to God, including any feelings of doubt.

Close by reading Psalm 77:10-15 responsively. In these verses David finds the strength and reassurance he needs in God.

OPTIONS

HANDOUT 3: EVERYBODY DOUBTS

Handout 3 offers a brief reading that supports the theme of today's meeting. You could distribute it just prior to the closing prayer, taking turns reading it aloud or having group members read it silently to themselves. After the reading, ask for questions or comments. You might ask if they've ever thought of Jesus as struggling with doubts.

Should you not have time to deal with the handout during the meeting, distribute it and encourage kids to read it at home for devotions this week.

TIME-SAVER

To save time on step 2, come to today's meeting with a number of magazine ads cut out and ready to distribute. Choose ads that have messages that are difficult to believe. Have kids work in pairs to tell what's difficult to believe about the ad. Discuss the results, then use the questions from step 2.

GUEST

Consider inviting a guest to come to speak to your group about his or her experience with doubts and questions. Select someone who will be able to relate well to high schoolers, someone whose experience will speak to their hearts (perhaps a new convert, or a person who has dealt with a handicap or the death of a loved one, or someone who has struggled to make a decision to profess his faith). Beforehand, be sure to explain the theme of today's meeting so that your guest can prepare his or her remarks in a way that will encourage your group.

MEETING 2
What Is Faith, Anyway?

SCRIPTURE

Matthew 19:16-22

TODAY'S THEME

Some of our doubts may stem from confusion about what faith is. In Mark 11:23 Jesus says, "I tell you the truth, if anyone says to this mountain, 'Go, throw yourself into the sea,' and does not doubt in his heart but believes that what he says will happen, it will be done for him."

The reality for most of us is that mountains are not jumping into the sea at our command. We aren't sure that we believe this verse. Does this make us doubters? Don't we possess enough faith? What is faith, anyway? Is it absolute certainty, confidence, and conviction all of the time? An important discovery comes when we realize the essence of faith isn't in intellectual knowledge but in a relationship with the living Christ.

Our will doesn't move mountains, but God's will does. And the way to discover God's will is through a loving relationship with him. What Jesus wants us to realize is that the life of faith—a life lived in intimate, prayerful communion with the Father—is eternal life. Uprooting a mountain and throwing it into the sea is a walk in the park compared to making those who are dead alive again.

This meeting focuses on what faith is, and on some common obstacles that keep our faith from growing.

GOALS OF THE MEETING

- to realize that faith is a vital part of our daily lives
- to describe what Jesus' encounter with a rich young man teaches us about faith
- to identify having a loving relationship with God as the key to faith
- to identify stumbling blocks that can get in the way of our faith

MATERIALS

1. Bibles
2. Handouts 4-6, pens or pencils
3. Several sheets of newsprint (or other large sheets of paper), markers

THEME THOUGHTS

At a Christian camp a young woman was considering whether to become a follower of Christ. She had listened all week to the gospel being presented in language she could understand. She was moving toward God, but she was hesitant. She wasn't sure of all the implications of this decision. She saw herself as very self-reliant and self-sufficient; the idea of giving control of her life to Christ, whom she couldn't see, hear, or feel, made her uneasy.

She shared her feelings with a friend who told her, "Christianity is like a course you sign up for at school. You kind of know what it is when you begin, but you really learn it as you go along."

This answer only increased the young woman's confusion. She wanted a road to walk down with sure footing, but her friend was inviting her to take a leap into mystery.

As Christians, how much sure footing do we really have? Hebrews 11:1 defines faith as the certainty of things not seen. Faith has also been described as belief that is not based on proof.

The young woman wanted certainty, but if there were a universally accepted proof of God's existence, then faith wouldn't be necessary. Faith isn't built around intellectual certainty but around a relationship of trust. It's been said that expecting a human to be able to prove God's existence is like expecting Mickey Mouse to be able to prove the existence of Walt Disney. The creature is unable to master the creator. The finite is unable to master the infinite.

We can't prove the existence of God, but we can experience God. Proving God's existence is like trying to convince someone that Niagara Falls is spectacular. We can talk about the height of the falls or the amount of water that pours over every second. Yet all our arguments may not convince our listener that the falls are spectacular. To do that, we need to stand with that person on the edge of the falls, to let him or her experience them.

The issue isn't so much whether we *believe in* God, but whether we *believe* God. Do we believe that he never leaves us? Do we believe he hears us when we pray? Do we believe that his grace is enough for us? Do we believe we are safe when we place our lives in his hands? Do we not only think these things are true but live as though they are?

It's one thing to think something is true, another thing to believe something is true. Belief is proved in action. That's why the book of James says that "faith without works is dead." Faith is God's great gift to us, lived out when we trust God and submit ourselves to his power.

John 17:3 says, "Now this is eternal life: that they may know you, the only true God, and Jesus Christ, whom you have sent." Eternal life comes through knowing. Another way to speak of "knowing" someone is to say we have a relationship with that person. Faith is not so much a thing to be accomplished as it is a relationship to be lived. Faith is yielding our will and desires into the hands of God.

During this meeting your group will explore faith, first through an exercise that illustrates the roles faith and trust play in daily living, and second, through looking at a contemporary version of the story of Jesus' encounter with a rich young man. The novelist F. Scott Fitzgerald once said that the rich are different from you and me. The point of this story is that they aren't. All of us struggle with placing our faith and trust in someone or something other than Christ. The rich young man's struggle is our struggle, because all of us are tempted to trust in ourselves and our own resources.

MEETING PLAN

1 A MEASURE OF FAITH
15-20 minutes

Distribute Handout 4 ("A Measure of Faith") and read the directions to the group:

Each activity listed below requires faith. How much faith? Read the list and then—working by yourself—rank the activities from 1 (takes the most faith) to 15 (takes the least faith). Put down what you think—there are no right or wrong answers.

Allow five minutes for completing the exercise. As a leader, you will want to do the exercise yourself. Some of the items may not appear at first glance to require much faith, but on reflection you will see that they do.

Lead the group into a discussion of the exercise. One way to organize the reporting is to ask each person to identify his or her number one item and his or her number fifteen item. Occasionally ask for people to say why they think an item would take a great deal of faith or less faith.

Ask the group to draw some conclusions about faith from the exercise. One that should be mentioned is that practically everything we do in life requires a certain amount of faith. Faith is essential to living.

Before going on, ask for some sample definitions of faith. Kids may mention trusting in someone or something, believing something is true without scientific proof, feeling or believing something in your heart, and so on. Receive each idea with appreciation. Ask the group to be open to other ideas about faith as we get further into today's meeting.

2 HOLDING ON TIGHTLY
15-20 minutes

Distribute Handout 5 ("Holding on Tightly"). This is a contemporary version of the familiar story of the rich young man (Matt. 19:16-22). We tell the story in this fashion to make it fresh and appealing, but also to provide background that shows the young man as much more than a greedy, one-dimensional character.

Take turns reading the story aloud. Do not reveal as yet that it's a retelling of a biblical story.

After reading the story, ask the group to turn to Matthew 19:16-22. Ask someone to read this passage aloud, then discuss the questions on the handout.

1. Brian is rich in material possessions. How would you describe him spiritually?

It would be a mistake to label him spiritually poor or dead. Brian is a decent, religious person, earnestly searching for God's answers to life. True, in the end he lacks the faith to accept those answers. But before we're too critical, we need to ask ourselves what we would have done in his place. The biblical story is so powerful precisely because we can see ourselves in it.

2. Jesus quotes some of the Ten Commandments. The first four commandments deal with our relationship with God, and the last six deal with our relationships with each other. Of the last six, which one does Jesus leave out (see Ex. 20)? Why do you think he omits this commandment?

Jesus skips the tenth commandment: "You shall not covet." Typically, we think of coveting as something like envy—wanting what someone else has. Coveting also means "to have excessive desires." Brian's struggle isn't wanting what someone else has—it's holding too tightly to what he has. Jesus clearly knows that as much as Brian wants to do something good, he can't, because his heart is set on his wealth. Brian loves being rich and, although he doesn't realize it, he has become a slave to his wealth.

3. Jesus adds the summary of the second half of the Ten Commandments: "Love others as much as you love yourself." Do you think Brian failed to do this? Why or why not?

Brian's love of money may be blinding him to the needs of others, especially the poor. Note, for example, his attitude toward the poor in Harlem. He believes they have "thrown their lives away," and they make him feel afraid and uncomfortable. Brian shows no evidence of compassion for the poor. He only wants to escape their presence.

Note that this detail is an addition to our contemporary story that's not directly paralleled in the biblical account. However, the rich young man in Matthew's account may also have been self-centered. He refuses to share his wealth with the poor, as the Lord told him to do.

4. What does Jesus ask Brian to do?

Most of us think first, like Brian, in terms of the amount of money Jesus asked Brian to give away. We tend to think, "Jesus asks Brian to give away all his money so he can have eternal life." But that borders on the kind of "works-righteousness" thinking that Brian demonstrates. The most significant thing in Jesus' encounter with Brian is his invitation to a relationship—"Come, follow me." Eternal life is not found in giving your money away; it's found in a relationship with Jesus Christ. That's the essence of faith.

This passage is misunderstood if it is looked at as a condemnation of wealth. The Bible is clear that God calls some people to be wealthy and to do wonderful things through the stewardship of their wealth. This passage is an illustration of the dangers of setting your heart on anything other than God.

5. Why does he refuse? Where does his faith ultimately lie?

He refuses to listen to Jesus because he places a greater value on his wealth than on his relationship with God.

In a sense his faith is in his money, in its power to buy whatever he needs or wants. Clearly, he loves being rich. We can also say, however, that his faith is in himself, in his own ability to make sense out of life, in his ability to *do* something to earn his own salvation. Even after rejecting Jesus' advice, perhaps he still hopes to find his own way to God. Although most of us cannot identify with someone who is a multimillionaire at the age of twenty-two, *all* of us can identify with placing our faith in our own abilities rather than in Christ.

6. What are your feelings about Brian?
  __ **I think he's stupid.**
  __ **He makes me mad.**
  __ **I feel sorry for him.**
  __ **I understand what he did.**
  __ **In some ways I can identify with him.**
  __ **Other:**_____

For each statement, ask for a show of hands from those who checked it. Ask one or two of those who checked a statement to give reasons for their choice.

7. In addition to money/wealth, what are some other things people hold onto that may keep them from trusting God?

You may want to work in groups of two to four people on this question. Give each group a sheet of newsprint on which to write their responses.

Encourage the groups not to settle for cliché answers, but to speak from their experience. To some degree or another, everyone places trust in something or someone other than God. Give the groups a couple of minutes to list their choices, then display the newsprint sheets and let the groups elaborate on their responses.

Maybe we believe that if we can get all As, then life will be good. Or we might think that having a relationship with a special person will make life work. Or things will be great if only we get our dream job, or our dream car, or if we make the team. We all seem to struggle with self-sufficiency. We seem to have an innate trust in our own abilities and intellect.

A more common problem than disbelief is disobedience. Some of us are blocked in our relationship with God because we do nothing to cultivate that relationship. Instead, we participate in behavior directly opposing the desires of God, and then wonder why we feel numb and have no sense of God's presence.

3 MARCEL THE MAGNIFICENT
10 - 15 minutes

Distribute Handout 6 ("Marcel the Magnificent"). Allow a couple of minutes for kids to read the parable themselves. Talk about what they think the parable says about faith. Point out (if the kids don't) that among the things the parable teaches is that faith is based on our relationship to a person. To ride the tightrope on Marcel's back would mean placing all your trust in him and in his ability to get you safely across the chasm.

Give everyone several minutes to complete the three statements about faith on the handout. Be sure to do the exercise yourself.

- **I have faith in Jesus because . . .**
- **Instead of putting my faith in God, sometimes I'm tempted to trust in . . .**
- **I want to grow in my faith by . . .**

When all are finished writing, invite anyone who wishes to do so to share one or more responses. Giving your own response to a statement or two may encourage kids to share their responses as well.

4 CANDLE PRAYER
5 minutes

Close today's session with a candle prayer. Gather in a circle, then take a candle and light it. Comment that one way to think of faith is as a light shining in the darkness.

Explain that you as leader will hold the candle for a few seconds, then pass it on to the next person. While each person holds the candle, the others should silently pray that God will increase this person's faith, and that his or her faith will light the way for others during the coming week.

OPTIONS

STORIES OF FAITH
Instead of the ranking exercise in step 1, have group members share stories of times when they really needed to have faith in someone (like a person's promise to repay a debt) or something (like a car starting late at night in a deserted parking lot).

Be prepared to tell your own story to get things started. After the stories, work on a definition of faith.

ACTS OF FAITH
As a follow-up activity to today's meeting, ask group members to perform one "act of faith" during the coming week. In other words, you're asking that they pledge to do something useful or helpful that requires faith (trust in God, a willingness to take a risk for the sake of doing something right, or a step into uncertainty). For example, someone might try talking about God with that friend at school who's not a Christian. Another person might ask God for guidance on some issue in his or her life, trusting God both to hear the prayer and to do what's best.

Add a measure of accountability by having them describe their plan to a partner. At your next meeting the partners can exchange stories of what they did.

PEOPLE OF FAITH
If your kids are familiar with the Bible, here's something you could try as a substitute for, or addition to, today's story about the rich young man (step 2).

Ask everyone to find a partner, then pantomime or dramatize a Bible story that shows faith. Partners may combine with other pairs to dramatize a story with several characters if they wish. After the presentations, talk about how the characters showed faith. You may want to suggest using Hebrews 11 as a source for names of persons of faith.

MEETING 3

Looking for Answers?

SCRIPTURE

Isaiah 42:3; John 14:1-7; 20:19-29

TODAY'S THEME

Does God want us to search for answers to our questions, or does he just want us to have faith that he knows what he's doing?

The best answer to both questions may be yes. There is a paradox here. As finite, human creatures, we will never understand everything. But that doesn't mean we shouldn't try. God gave us our minds to use.

Because mystery lies at the heart of the Christian faith, sometimes we downplay the reasons for our faith. In the eighteenth century, Samuel Johnson complained of a theologian who "tended to unsettle every thing, and yet settle nothing." First Peter 3:15 advises us to "always be prepared to give an answer to everyone who asks you to give the reason for the hope that you have."

There are answers to the questions doubters raise. Knowing the answers can produce confidence and conviction, and strengthen our lives as followers of Christ.

GOALS OF THE MEETING

- to realize that while our faith ultimately rests in Christ, there are answers for our questions about God and the life of faith
- to provide "answers" to an emotional and an intellectual challenge to the Christian faith
- to describe the questions/doubts Thomas raised
- to raise some questions/doubts of our own and begin to address them

MATERIALS

1. Bibles
2. Handouts 7-9, pens or pencils
3. List of questions to ask Jesus (from Meeting 1)
4. Notecards

THEME THOUGHTS

Here is a simple but profound story: One night a man was searching for something under a streetlight. Another man came by and asked him what he had lost.

"I dropped my house key."

"You dropped your house key out here, in the street?"

"No, I dropped it up by the door. But the light is better here."

Where do we look for the answers to what troubles us? Do we look in places where it is easy to look, but where we don't have a chance of finding what we're after? It's sad when people ask tough questions but settle for the easy and often misguided answers supplied by our secular culture. It's sad too when people abandon the search for answers after only a brief and superficial search.

Our serious questions should be pursued to the end. Tim Stafford writes, "The walls of Christian faith are not so thin that you will break holes in them by pushing too hard. If you ask honestly, you will find answers—though not always the answers you would have liked."

"Seek and you shall find," Jesus promises. "Knock and the door shall be opened."

In the Bible honest doubters are not condemned but answered frankly—from the tortured questioning of Job to the "show me" skepticism of Thomas. God's anger doesn't fall on doubters; it falls on those who already "know all the answers" and presume to speak for God. So we should boldly state what concerns us and search for answers.

And yet, we also need to remember that the Christian faith is full of mystery. John Calvin said that there are some mysteries he'd rather adore and experience than try to explain: "My mind can conceive more than my tongue can express, and these things are beyond what my mind can conceive."

In this meeting your group will look at a couple of examples of young people with questions, and they'll be asked to answer those questions. Next, the group will be looking at Thomas, perhaps the most famous doubter in the Bible, and identifying ways to seek answers to troubling questions. And finally, they will begin to deal with some of their own questions.

MEETING PLAN

1 ANY MORE QUESTIONS?
5 minutes

Begin by explaining that today we'll be looking at some of the questions and doubts we have about our faith. Remind the group that a couple of weeks ago, we wrote down some of the questions we would like to ask Jesus. If you recorded those questions on newsprint, tape the newsprint sheet to your wall or otherwise display it for reference later in the meeting.

Distribute notecards and invite kids to jot down any additional questions they'd like to add to the list, including more general questions they might have about their faith. Any sincere question is welcome. Names need not be signed to the cards.

After several minutes, collect the cards and put them aside for use in step 3.

2 DOUBTING THOMAS
20 minutes

Distribute Bibles and take turns reading John 14:1-7, where we are introduced to Thomas, the honest and blunt asker of questions. Also take turns reading John 20:19-29, where Thomas seeks convincing evidence that Jesus has really risen from the dead.

Distribute Handout 7 ("Doubting Thomas") for Frederick Buechner's look at Thomas. We suggest you read this aloud to the group. Practice it at home a couple of times so you can read it smoothly as the kids follow on their copy.

Use the questions at the end of the handout to discuss Doubting Thomas. Guidelines follow:

1. **Re-read Buechner's description of Thomas in the first paragraph. Imagine having a friend like Thomas. What would he be like? Fill in some details. Would you enjoy having this kind of friend? Why or why not?**

Buechner paints Thomas as a no-nonsense kind of guy, someone who is interested in just the facts and nothing but the facts. He is a realist who probably wishes Jesus wouldn't speak in riddles so often. He is blunt and honest.

Let the kids fill in some details of a modern-day Thomas. If necessary, ask questions like these: What kind of TV shows would he enjoy? Dislike? What kind of car would he drive? What would he be like in class? And so on.

Would they enjoy having a friend like this? A modern-day Thomas might be something of a cynic—he might come up a bit short on the fun and the imaginative. On the other hand, he'd be real. He'd let you know where he stood on just about anything.

2. Give three examples that show Thomas's realistic (non-imaginative, skeptical) nature.

Encourage the kids to use both Scripture and Buechner's retelling. First, we see Thomas—and only Thomas—bluntly telling Jesus that what he said about "knowing the way" puzzled him. That takes a fair amount of courage—the other disciples (or even Jesus) might think him stupid or arrogant. But that doesn't stop Thomas. When he has a question, he asks it.

And then there's his infamous doubting the other disciples' claim that they actually saw Jesus. "No way I'll believe without seeing and touching the evidence for myself," says Thomas, thereafter to be remembered by the world as Doubting Thomas.

A third instance of Thomas' realistic nature may be harder to pinpoint, but here's an example. Unlike the other disciples, who are locked in a room "imagining the horrors that were all too likely in store for themselves," Thomas is roaming around, maybe "out for a cup of coffee." He's out on his own, trying to make sense of everything that's happened.

3. How does Jesus deal with Doubting Thomas? What does this say to you about the way Jesus deals with our doubts?

Jesus could have been furious at Thomas's hardheaded skepticism. Or he could have avoided Thomas, letting him stew in his doubts. Instead, he deliberately goes to Thomas, and without being asked, offers Thomas the proof he seeks. And then follows a high point of faith, a beautiful confession: "My Lord and my God!" Thomas has come home. True, Jesus reserves a special blessing for those who believe without the benefit of "seeing." Yet he doesn't hesitate to reach out in love to his doubting disciple.

For us in all our doubts and questions, this is good news!

4. Jesus says, "Blessed are those who have not seen and yet believe." Do you agree with Buechner that "it's hard to imagine a believer anywhere who wouldn't have traded places with Thomas, given the chance"? Would you? Explain.

Solicit some honest reactions. As followers of Jesus who are often filled with our own doubts and questions, the idea of seeing and touching the risen Savior, of knowing firsthand that the resurrection is an absolute fact, is appealing. Perhaps some of us, like Thomas, long for that sort of "proof."

Yet Jesus says we're blessed if we believe without that sort of proof. The great point to stress is that we can know in our hearts that the resurrection is true, just as surely as Thomas knew after he saw Jesus. This is what faith can do for us.

The other thing to remember is that not all who see actually believe. Scientific "proof" isn't as powerful as the simple faith created by the Spirit in our hearts.

5. Since we can't trade places with Thomas, what can we do? List some concrete steps you can take to find answers to whatever puzzles you about the Christian faith.

This may seem simplistic, but it goes back to the opening illustration about searching for the lost key. The best way to find answers is to openly ask our questions of someone who can probably answer them.

Too often we keep our doubts in our hearts without letting others share them. Ask a pastor. Ask a youth worker. Ask a friend. Ask a parent. Ask God. Just ask!

Also, we can read what other thinkers have written. There are plenty of good resources available to help us. And we can enter the study of Scripture in a renewed way. It's been said, "The Bible does not yield its secrets to the casual or flippant reader." One of the great challenges of working with youth is to help them fall in love with the Scriptures.

We can also direct kids to the historic creeds and confessions of the church. Some youth leaders may choke on this suggestion, because too often the creeds have been used to bore kids into a kind of stagnant submission that robs our faith of its dynamic qualities. But the creeds articulate what the church has believed over time. As with Scripture, kids need time-tested truth, not just the latest fads and clichés. As leaders, our challenge is to help bring these historic documents alive in fresh ways, so that their truth will speak to this generation.

3 SITUATIONS
20-30 minutes

Distribute Handout 8 ("Situations"), and divide the group into pairs. Ask half the pairs to deal with Jenny's situation, the other half with Mark's. Give each pair five minutes to read the story and jot down their responses.

While the pairs are working, look over the notecards you collected at the beginning of the meeting. Use a sheet of newsprint to jot down additional questions the group could discuss later in this step. We hope that discussing the two situations will prepare the kids to talk about their own questions and doubts. Perhaps some of their questions and concerns can be dealt with during your discussion of the two situations. Do save some time at the end of this step to deal with at least a couple of the kids' personal questions.

Ask each pair to present their responses to Jenny's and Mark's situations. Remind the group that while there may not be final, once-and-for-all answers to Jenny's and Mark's questions, there are answers that have satisfied people throughout human history. You may want to recommend some resources like C. S. Lewis's *Mere Christianity* or *The Screwtape Letters*.

The following thoughts may help you lead the discussion. The important thing here is not to give airtight answers to these situations, but to allow the kids to struggle with stating what they believe.

Some thoughts about Jenny's struggles
It is hard to imagine that God loves us when we don't feel loved by anyone around us. Jenny's questions are more emotional than intellectual. So an appropriate response to Jenny would be to simply be a good friend to her—to listen, love, pray, and be with her. Help your group realize that a primary way we experience God's love is through other people.

Jenny's story also raises the question of why pain and suffering exist. You may want to remind the group that one of the greatest expressions of how much God loves us is the freedom he allows us to make choices. Sometimes the choices we make don't honor God or show love and compassion to others. Sometimes there is no clear path, and innocent people will be hurt no matter what choice we make.

Most of us don't have a very good theology of suffering. We believe that our status as followers of Christ should somehow make us immune from pain. The reality is that pain and suffering exist for every human, and that even Jesus experienced deep pain. God's heart breaks when we hurt each other. As Christians our hope is not that we won't experience pain, but that a time will come when "God will wipe away all tears" (Revelation 21:4).

Some thoughts about Mark's struggles
Mark's questions are more intellectual in nature. Apparently they have not been prompted by a crisis or by loneliness. Mark simply wonders what reasons there are for believing God exists.

The first is the reality of our own experience, which may not be dramatic or radical but is authentic. You may want to mention the example of the blind man in John 9 whom Jesus cured. After he was healed, the Pharisees engaged him in a theological discussion about what happened to him. Blind from birth, this man most likely had no education, and so we might expect him to be intimidated by these learned men. Yet the man could clearly state one unarguable fact with great conviction: "One thing I do know. I was blind but now I see!" (John 9:25).

What other evidence is there of God's existence? Think of the complexity of creation. So much of the universe defies explanation. From the farthest reaches of space to the tiniest subatomic particles, the universe is ordered in infinite and unfathomable ways. For this reason, many have concluded that there must be a creator.

The existence of the church thousands of years after the death of Christ is another reason for believing in the reality of God. Even a quick study of church history reveals plenty of good reasons for the church *not* to exist. The only possible explanation for why the church has survived persecution from the outside and corruption from within is God. God has used imperfect people and institutions to carry the message of his perfect love and redemption.

These thoughts are a beginning, but they are hardly exhaustive. You may also want to distribute and discuss Handout 9 ("If There Really Is a God").

What does Isaiah 42:3 tell us about God's attitude toward people like Jenny and Mark?

In some ways, Jenny is a "bruised reed" and Mark a "dimly burning wick." God deals tenderly with those that are hurt and honestly with those who doubt.

Pause and make the transition to the questions that group members wrote on the notecards (or that are left over from the first meeting). Try to reach a consensus on one or two questions that they would like to talk about for a few minutes. If they're interested in discussing other questions of faith, set aside some time for this during the next meeting, or arrange an extra meeting or two for this purpose.

4 CLOSING
5 minutes

Remind the group that when we reason about God, there's always a danger of losing Christ and believing instead in our own arguments. Our faith should be reasonable and rational, not unreasonable and irrational. But in its fullest expression, faith is found in a warm, dynamic relationship with Jesus Christ.

John Calvin said that although reason is a "natural gift," it is so "weakened and corrupted" that only "misshapen ruins appear." When it comes to what "human reason can discern with regard to God's kingdom and spiritual insight," the "greatest geniuses are blinder than moles"!

Suggest that we focus for a few minutes on the mystery and awesomeness of God. Begin by reading responsively Isaiah's beautiful description of the mystery and power and love of God (Isa. 40:21-31).

After the reading, give people an opportunity to praise God, perhaps by completing this statement: "Dear God, I praise you for . . ." During the time of silence between prayers, group members may focus on God's greatness and love.

Close your prayer time by reflecting on our relationship to Jesus Christ. Reading Psalm 23 responsively is one way to do this.

OPTIONS

THE UNBELIEVING GUEST
As an extension of this meeting, you could invite someone you know who is not a Christian to speak to your group, explaining his or her reasons for not accepting Christianity.

The guest would need to be told to expect questions from the group, and the group should be reminded to treat the guest with courtesy and tact.

You'll need to decide if your group is mature enough to handle this option. It's probably best to use with a group of older teens (seniors in high school) who are fairly secure in their faith. It's also wise to send a letter to each group member's home explaining what you've planned and why. In fact, you may want to invite parents to attend the meeting too.

TIME-SAVER
Instead of using Handout 8 ("Situations") for step 3, proceed immediately to the questions kids wrote on the notecards (and those that are left over from Meeting 1). This, of course, assumes that you've collected enough questions to discuss. A more likely problem is having too many questions to deal with. Try to reach a consensus on which ones the kids would most like to discuss.

HANDOUT 9: IF THERE REALLY IS A GOD . . .
This *Campus Life* article by Ruth Senter makes an excellent follow-up to today's meeting. It reviews some common reasons for not believing in God, then offers a number of strong arguments for believing in God. Distribute the handout and ask group members to read it at home.

If you have time during today's session, you could distribute Handout 9 at the end of step 3. Give kids a few minutes to read the handout, then ask for reactions.

MEETING 4
What's Our Focus?

SCRIPTURE

Matthew 14:22-33

TODAY'S THEME

The compelling thing about Christianity is not that it is good, or nice, or better than other religions, but that it is true. What can bring us to state this simple fact with conviction?

Reportedly, the first steamship to cross the Atlantic Ocean carried on board a copy of a book that "proved" that steamships couldn't carry enough fuel to cross the ocean. We don't know for sure what the book's author had to say after the historic crossing, but it's safe to assume he said something like, "Oops!"

History is full of skeptics who have been proven wrong, from the people who were certain Columbus would sail off the edge of the flat earth to those who repeatedly said, "It'll never fly" to the Wright brothers.

What about doubting God? There are honest reasons to doubt. Every tragedy that strikes humanity—every plane crash, every case of cancer, every drive-by shooting, every war—creates doubt by providing surface evidence that God is absent, not present.

What does it take to believe in the face of these tragedies? What should we do with our doubts? Today's meeting reminds us all to keep our eyes on Jesus, to make him the center of our faith.

GOALS OF THE MEETING

- to recognize experience and knowledge as ways of overcoming doubt
- to describe what we can learn about faith and doubt from the example of Peter walking with Jesus on the waves
- to identify specific ways to focus on Jesus
- to commit to implementing one of these ways

MATERIALS

1. Bibles
2. Handouts 10-11, pens or pencils
3. Several sheets of newsprint (or other large sheets of paper), markers
4. Large white candle, matches
5. Notecards
6. Flashlight (optional)

THEME THOUGHTS

On October 20, 1995, two special people named Art and Jean celebrated their fiftieth wedding anniversary. A couple of days later Art was asked if he had any doubts that Jean was the right person for him.

"No doubt at all," he said.

"Did you have any doubt fifty years ago?"

"Fifty years ago I thought Jean was the right person. Today I know."

What moved Art from *thinking* the decision he and Jean were making was right to *knowing* it was right? It was experience. Fifty years of experience. Fifty years spent raising four children and watching eleven grandchildren grow. Fifty years of being there for each other—of Art being there for Jean as she overcame cancer and, a few years later, of Jean being there for Art as he overcame cancer. Experience erases doubt.

So it is with our relationship with God. As we experience God consistently over time, our doubts fade. It's been said that most people start with Christianity and only gradually grow to know Christ. Eventually, we will see Christ. "Now we see but a poor reflection as in a mirror," Paul says in 1 Corinthians 13, "then we shall see face to face." There will come a time when we will say "farewell to shadowlands," to use C. S. Lewis's phrase. In the presence of Christ, our questions and doubts will be irrelevant.

We live in the hope of that time, but we are not there yet. How do we grow when our feelings change and our faith seems to go up and down?

One of the keys to growing in Christ is direction. In this final meeting, the group will consider how knowledge and experience help increase faith and decrease doubt. A deep experience of God is more likely to come to those who are focused on him. We'll look at Peter and see what difference focus and direction made to Peter when he walked on water to join Jesus.

MEETING PLAN

1 TWO TRUTHS AND A LIE
10 minutes

This is a fun game! Give everyone a few minutes to think of three things they can share about themselves. Two of the "facts" should be true; one should be false. Each person then shares his or her statements with the rest of the group. Group members guess which statement is false. This is just for fun—no "winners" or "losers," please.

After the game, ask what factors helped identify the false statements. Conclude with the group that one factor is how well we know the person making the statement. Generally, the better we know someone, the easier it is to guess what is true and what isn't.

Ask how this applies to our relationship with God. The better we know God, the more "experience" we have with God, the easier it is to rely on him and trust him. Knowledge and experience go a long way toward increasing our faith and decreasing our doubt.

2 WIND, WAVES, AND FOCUS
20-25 minutes

Tell the group that our Bible study for today will focus on something extremely unusual that happened to Peter. Comment that Peter was one of the most interesting characters around Jesus. At times he could be impulsive, dumb, and cowardly (as when he denied Christ). At other times he could be thoughtful, wise, and brave (as when he preached on Pentecost and later went to prison for his faith). In other words, Peter was a real person, a mixture of good and bad and everything in between.

Ask the group to find Matthew 14:22-33. You may want to read this passage as "reader's theater," asking group members to read the lines of the various characters. You will need

- a narrator (reads everything not in quotation marks)
- disciples (several kids read the two lines of the disciples in unison)
- Peter
- Jesus

If you prefer, simply read the passage aloud with expression yourself.

After the reading, break into small groups of two to four people. Give each group a sheet of newsprint and a marker. Ask the groups to re-read the passage carefully and to jot down what it teaches us about faith and doubt. Encourage them to write as many ideas down as possible. Give them an example if you think they need it. Allow no more than ten minutes for the groups to complete this exercise.

Call the groups together to display their sheet of newsprint and to report their conclusions. Let them know by your positive comments and attitude that you value their insights into the passage. Here are some ideas that you may want to raise if the groups don't mention them on their own.

- Like the disciples, we'll have some dark and stormy nights in our lives. We'll be afraid. Our faith will be tested.
- Sometimes we'll be confident and strong in our faith; sometimes we'll be doubting and weak. Look at Peter. He was bold enough to leave the safety of the boat and walk toward Jesus. But then his faith wavered and he began to sink.
- Sometimes we may have to take some risks for our faith. Like Peter, we have to be willing to take that first, dangerous step toward Jesus.
- Our faith is strong when we look to Jesus, when we focus on him. Peter didn't know if he would sink or walk on water. He simply kept looking at Jesus, trusting in him. As long as he stayed focused on Jesus, he could do the impossible.
- As soon as we lose our focus on Jesus, we lose our faith. Ask when Peter first began to sink. Why then and not earlier? Peter sank when he noticed the wind. He had been walking toward Jesus over the waves, but when he realized what he was doing and heard the wind and saw the waves, he became afraid, began to sink, and cried out for help. He lost his focus on Jesus, and his doubts overcame him.
- Fear can cause us to lose our focus on Jesus. Ask what kinds of things we might be afraid of. Expand the idea to include other things, good and bad, that could distract us from Christ (sports, money, temptation, success, work, and the like).
- When we do start sinking (doubting, losing our faith), Jesus cares. He will not let us drown in our doubt. He gave his life for us. He won't let us go.

---

3 FOCUSED ON JESUS

10 minutes

Quickly return to the same small groups as the previous step. This time, give the groups five minutes to list some things we can do that help us remain focused on Jesus. These should be things that have actually worked for them or for someone they know. They can be positive ("Do this . . . ") or negative ("Avoid doing this . . . "). The groups can make their lists on the opposite side of the newsprint sheets used for the previous exercise (save some paper!).

Review the complete lists with the groups. Below are a few comments you may want to work into the discussion:

- We need to focus on "whatever is true, whatever is noble, whatever is right, whatever is pure . . . " (Phil. 4:8). "Garbage in, garbage out" applies to computers but also to our lives. When we fill our lives with the garbage of violence and sex through the movies we watch and the music we listen to, when we live for the things we can buy, when we resort to alcohol or drugs for a high, is it any wonder that we feel distant from God? The modern word for these behaviors is *unhealthy*. The biblical word that describes them is *sin*.
- We need to make time for personal devotions. In Matthew 6:7-8, Christ quite clearly expects his followers to spend time in prayer. One great way to encourage the members of your group to develop a rich prayer life is through journaling. Encourage them to write down their prayers regularly and to review what they've written from time to time. They will begin to see more clearly that God hears and answers their prayers.

Talk about how devotions are tools for encouraging our faith. If they become a series of shame-filled, missed obligations, then we are trying to perform something alien to us. Help kids discover grace and encouragement. You may want to ask your group members for ideas that have helped make their personal devotions more meaningful and enjoyable. If this whole area is a struggle for your group, consider ways to spend some extended time helping liberate kids to spend regular, enjoyable time with God.

- We need to take time to worship with God's people. True, for some young people the regular service of their church does not provide meaningful worship. It's unrealistic to expect kids to suddenly become adults or the worship service to suddenly become "kid friendly." There should be some movement in both directions. Youth leaders can help by working with kids to create age-appropriate worship opportunities. You may want to brainstorm some "I wish our services . . ." statements with the group.
- We need to be an active part of the Christian community. "By this everyone will know that you are my disciples, if you love one another" (John 13:35). All believers, including kids, benefit from regular experiences in groups where they can be both genuine and loved.
- We need to serve. One of the best prescriptions for a doubt-filled person is to actively serve God by serving others. Neil Plantinga writes, "A kindness offered to someone else's need is twice blessed. It helps the person to whom it is offered. And it helps us who offer it." Invite group members who have participated in some service projects to tell how serving helped them focus on Jesus.

4 CLOSING
10 minutes

Distribute notecards (one each) to group members, including yourself. Invite them to jot down one way they will attempt to stay focused on Jesus this week. It could be an act of service or a commitment to pray each day or a promise to avoid a certain behavior that distracts them from Jesus. Assure them that if they make a commitment, it will remain private, between them and God (an option for close-knit groups is to share their commitment with a partner, who will pray for them during the week). Wait until all who wish to participate have written something on their cards.

Then darken the room as much as possible, and light a single large candle. Ask the group to gather around the candle. Take your Bible and read Isaiah 9:2 and John 8:12 to the group (you may need a flashlight for this).

> *The people walking in darkness have seen a great light; on those living in the land of the shadow of death a light has dawned.*

> *When Jesus spoke again to the people, he said, "I am the light of the world. Whoever follows me will never walk in darkness, but will have the light of life."*

Remind your group of our need to keep our eyes on Jesus, to stay focused on the light of the world. Invite them to pray silently that God will help them carry out the commitment they've just written down. Invite those who have not chosen to write a commitment to simply focus on Jesus as the one who offers the light of life.

Close the prayer yourself. Thank God for the faith displayed by each person, and ask for grace for all of us to keep our eyes on Jesus.

After the prayer, distribute Handout 11 (evaluation form) and ask everyone to complete it. There's also an evaluation form for you to fill out at the end of this leader's guide. We appreciate your effort in completing it so that we can better serve your needs in the future.

OPTIONS

HANDOUT 10: WHAT GOOD IS FAITH?

This *Campus Life* article by Jim Long presents one person's struggle to understand God "when life doesn't seem as good as we expect it to be."

If time permits, have kids read the article after today's Bible study in step 2. Ask for reactions to the answers the author arrives at. Do your group members find them helpful? Talk too about how knowledge and experience played a part in the author's response—note especially how he found "something to sink his faith into" in the Bible. Jan's observation from her hospital bed—"all the dots on the ceiling are people ... they all need Jesus ... "—reinforces our meeting's theme of staying focused on Jesus.

If you don't have time to deal with the handout during the meeting, distribute it at the end of the meeting for reading at home. A few words of endorsement from you may encourage your teens to read this honest and helpful piece.

CLOSING PRAYER

Here's a substitute for using the candle and accompanying passages. After group members fill out their commitment cards, ask them to close their eyes and to picture Jesus walking across the sea toward them, to hear him invite them to walk out to him, to keep their eyes on him while they leave the safety of the boat and walk to Jesus.

Then ask that they silently ask Jesus for help in keeping their commitment to stay focused on him this week.

Close the prayer time by telling the group that Jesus says to them: "Take courage! It is I. Don't be afraid. ... Come [to me]" (Matt. 14:27, 29).

VIDEO

If your group appreciated the *Campus Life* articles found in Handouts 9 and 10, you may want to order a three-part discussion video that further explores the roles of faith and doubt. You could use the video for additional sessions, for a retreat, or possibly for a meeting with parents and kids.

The video is produced by Camfel Productions in association with *Campus Life* magazine. *Campus Life* recommends the video for youth groups, church school classes, and Christian clubs. Cost is $24.95. To order, call 1-800-866-6464. Ask for the "Radical View" video for April/May/June and July/August of 1995. Mention product #RV003 and key code #VS5A13.

YES, NO, MAYBE SO: DEALING WITH DOUBT

Leader Evaluation Form

BACKGROUND

Size of group:
☐ under 5
☐ 5-10
☐ 10-15
☐ over 15

School grade of participants:
☐ grade 10
☐ grade 11
☐ grade 12
☐ post-high

Length of group sessions:
☐ under 30 minutes
☐ 30-45 minutes
☐ 45-60 minutes
☐ over 60 minutes

Please check items that describe you:
☐ male
☐ female
☐ ordained or professional church staff
☐ elder or deacon
☐ professional teacher
☐ church school or catechism teacher (three or more years)
☐ youth group leader

HANDOUTS FOR GROUP MEMBERS

In general, I
☐ did not use the handouts
☐ used the handouts frequently

Please check items that describe the handouts:
☐ too few
☐ too many
☐ helpful
☐ not helpful

LEADER'S GUIDE AND GROUP PROCESS

Please check the items that describe the activities suggested for each group session:
☐ varied
☐ monotonous
☐ creative
☐ dull
☐ clear
☐ unclear
☐ interesting to participants
☐ uninteresting to participants
☐ too many
☐ too few

Please check the items that describe the Theme Thoughts provided in the leader's guide:
☐ helpful, stimulating
☐ not helpful or stimulating
☐ overly complex, long
☐ about right level of difficulty
☐ clear
☐ unclear

The course in general was true to the Reformed/Presbyterian tradition.
☐ agree
☐ disagree
☐ not sure

Please check those procedures that worked best for you:
☐ small group discussions
☐ whole group discussions
☐ handouts
☐ use of session options
☐ other (please write in)

_____
_____
_____

Please check the items that describe the group sessions:
- [ ] lively
- [ ] dull
- [ ] dominated by leader
- [ ] involved most participants
- [ ] relevant to lives of participants
- [ ] irrelevant to lives of participants
- [ ] worthwhile
- [ ] not worthwhile

In general I would rate this material as
- [ ] excellent
- [ ] good
- [ ] fair
- [ ] poor

Additional comments on any aspect of this program:

_____
Name (optional)

_____
Church

_____
City/State/Province

Please send completed form to

LifeWise
CRC Publications
2850 Kalamazoo Ave. SE
Grand Rapids, Michigan 49560

Thank you!

Other available titles in the LifeWise series are

Gotta Have It: It's a Stewardship Thing

Not Everybody's Doing It: Making Choices About Sex

911: Calling for Help in a Violent World

Every Night Live: Making Choices About TV